Anonymous

Letters to a Member of the Present Parliament, upon the Extraordinary and Unprecedented Transactions in the Last House of Commons

Anonymous

Letters to a Member of the Present Parliament, upon the Extraordinary and Unprecedented Transactions in the Last House of Commons

ISBN/EAN: 9783744715843

Printed in Europe, USA, Canada, Australia, Japan

Cover: Foto ©ninafisch / pixelio.de

More available books at **www.hansebooks.com**

LETTERS

TO A

MEMBER

OF THE

PRESENT PARLIAMENT,

UPON THE EXTRAORDINARY AND
UNPRECEDENTED TRANSACTIONS

IN THE LAST

HOUSE OF COMMONS.

———————

LONDON:

Printed for J. DEBRETT, oppofite Burlington-Houfe, Piccadilly. 1784.

L E T T E R S,

&c. &c. &c.

L E T T E R I.

DEAR SIR,

IT has given me great satisfaction to find that you are elected a member of the new Parliament. That persons of an independant fortune, and who have been at pains to improve the advantages of a liberal education, should early acquire a knowledge of our Constitution, and take an active part in the government, is devoutly to be wished by every lover of his country. Give me leave to say, that your promising abilities, and the spirit you have hitherto discovered, encourage me to hope that, in the situation in which you are now placed, your conduct will be such as to reflect

B   honor

honor upon yourfelf and your connections. You are, indeed, beginning your political career at a very critical period ; when the proceedings of Parliament are likely to draw the attention of all Europe, and when its refolutions will not only afcertain decifively the character of its members, but probably determine the fate of a Conftitution, which has long been the boaft of Englifhmen, as well as the admiration and envy of their neighbours. The defire you exprefs of knowing my opinion, concerning the ftate of our public affairs, is highly flattering to me ; and I fhall take the liberty of communicating, without referve, fuch thoughts as I am unable to fupprefs on the prefent alarming crifis.

In order to form a right judgment of the feveral queltions which are now likely to be agitated, it feems neceffary that you fhould take a retrofpective view of the public occurrences for feveral months paft, and examine the courfe of events which has led to the diffolution of the former, and given birth to the prefent Parliament. Permit me, therefore, to recall to your memory a few of thofe particulars; from which the conduct of the different parties, the principles upon which they have acted, and the defigns which they are profecuting, will appear in the fulleft light.

In a review of this kind, the extraordinary circumftances attending the late change of Miniftry,

as

as they afford a key to the succeeding transactions, appear to demand your first attention. The interference of the Crown, with all its weight, to influence the determination of an important question then depending in the House of Peers, was undoubtedly an unconstitutional measure of the first magnitude. The vehement manner in which this was executed, the direct and even threatening intimation that was given concerning the inclinations of Majesty, leave no doubt about the intention of the measure: The success which attended it, renders its consequences truly alarming.

That the King, during the dependance of a bill, shall not take notice of the proceedings of either House, is a maxim obviously founded upon the separate departments belonging to the different branches of the Legislature, and which is manifestly essential to the freedom of debate, and to the independance of Parliament. There is accordingly no point, with respect to which parliament has been more watchful of its privileges, or has discovered greater jealousy of whatever might have the appearance of the least encroachment upon the part of the Crown *. The flagrant violation of

B 2   parliamentary

* See the proceedings of the House of Commons collected by Hatsell. This author mentions two exceptions to the maxim above-mentioned. The first where the King is interested

parliamentary privileges, in this particular, has
always been regarded as an indelible ſtain upon
the otherwiſe fortunate and glorious reign of Queen
Elizabeth : And it was a meaſure of the ſame ſort
which marked, in ſtrong characters, the diſſimu-
lation and tyrannical principles of the infatuated
Charles the Firſt.

I fancy you will agree with me in thinking,
that the appointment of the preſent Miniſters was
not ſo properly a *conſequence*, as it was a *part* of the
late tranſaction which I have mentioned.   There
can be no doubt that the whole plan was laid with
their advice and concurrence ; that they approved
of it in all its branches, and that their coming into
office, was a neceſſary and preconcerted link in the
ſcheme.   It cannot therefore be denied, that they
are reſponſible for this, as well as for every ſucceed-
ing meaſure of the Crown.

The reſolutions of the Houſe of Commons,
which followed this tranſaction, were ſuch as the
circumſtances of the caſe loudly demanded.   Had
the repreſentatives of the nation allowed themſelves
to wink at ſuch extraordinary proceedings, or
paſſed them over in ſilence, they would have been
juſtly conſidered as callous to every inſult upon

terected as a party, having a pecuniary intereſt. The ſecond,
on applications for public money. It will not, ſurely, be pretended that the late interference of the Crown, falls within
either of theſe exceptions.

their

their own dignity, as betraying the truft repofed in them by their Conftituents, and as tamely aban-doning the moft important rights of the people.

It was not poffible, at the fame time, to condemn thefe proceedings, without cenfuring the perfons who had been chiefly inftrumental in the execution of them. It was not poffible to condemn the crime, and with the fame breath to approve of the criminal ; far lefs to cherifh and reward him, or to employ him in thofe important departments which require the higheft national confidence.

The ftrong cenfures expreffed by the Houfe of Commons againft the advifers of this meafure, and the repeated addreffes which they carried to the Throne, for the removal of the prefent Miniftry, have given rife to a queftion the moft important, perhaps, of any that can be agitated with refpect to the Britifh Conftitution. That the Crown has the fole right of naming its Minifters, is indifputable. But is this right to be exercifed, in all cafes, without any fort of limitation or controul ? Is it not neceffary that Minifters fhall have the confidence of Parliament ? in particular, that they fhall have the confidence of the Houfe of Commons, by whom the fupplies are granted, and committed to the immediate direction of Miniftry ? And if the Re-prefentatives of the nation fhall entertain a fuf-picion, from whatever caufe, of the perfons appointed by the Crown for that purpofe, and fhall think

think them unfit for the truft committed to them, is it not the duty of the executive power to remove them from their offices? This is a queftion which every Englifhman ought ferioufly to confider; as it involves, not the intereft of this or that political party, but the deareft and moft important rights of the nation. The determination of this point appears to me to decide, whether we are to remain in the condition of a free people, or to be reduced under an abfolute government.

According to the fyftem of government eftablifhed at the Revolution, by which a proper line was drawn between the prerogative of the Crown and the privileges of the People, the Legiflative power, including that of impofing taxes, was vefted in the three branches of parliament ; and it was underftood that, in conformity to the ancient Conftitution, the particular fhare of the Legiflature, committed to the Crown, fhould be exercifed, in the way of a *negative* only, to fuch bills as might be paffed in the two Houfes. Such was the diftribution of the pre-eminent and controuling power in the State, which, at that glorious æra of our hiftory, received the fanction of public authority, and was intended to remain inviolable to future ages. The fettlement, which was made at that period, is to be confidered as the great ftandard, for afcertaining the nature of our limited monarchy. It is the fixed ftar which we, o. this ifland,

ought

ought never to lose fight of in all the mazes of political speculation. The rights of the Sovereign and of the people were then balanced with such peculiar propriety, that no superiority of power could afterwards be acquired by either party, without being fatal to that mixed form of government which it had been the general intention to secure.

The natural course of things, however, and the almost unavoidable modes of conducting public business, have, since that period, produced considerable deviations from the strict form of the Revolution settlement: but these deviations have been invariably of such a nature as to preserve the spirit and the essence of that happy establishment. If any new powers have been assumed by one party, which might seem an incroachment upon the rights of the other, these have been counterbalanced by a dereliction of other powers, or by the exercise of privileges upon the other side, from which the general equilibrium has been maintained, and the system of our liberties has remained upon its former basis.

Thus the unquestionable prerogative of refusing the Royal assent to bills which have passed the two Houses of Parliament, appears to be in a great measure relinquished; since only one instance of its exertion is to be found from the period above-mentioned; that is, during the course

of

of near a century. On the other hand, the Crown has, during the fame courfe of time, been accuftomed to the regular exercife of another branch of power, in reality of much greater con-fequence; that of *introducing*, by its Minifters, the greater part of bills which come under the deliberation of Parliament. It is now regarded as a fingularity, when debates of. a public nature, and in matters of importance, originate from a different quarter. In place of a mere negative, in the laft inftance, upon the refolutions of that affembly, the Crown has thus acquired the means of fuggefting every fubject of deliberation. In-ftead of interpofing a reftraint upon any innova-tion, it has in this manner become the prime mover of new regulations. From furnifhing merely the ballaft, it now fills the fails of the veffel.

This however is not the only alteration which time has introduced in the. partition of the great powers of government. It is well known that in ordinary cafes, the miniftry are accuftomed, not only to *bring in*, but to *carry through*, thofe bills which are agreeable to the wifhes of the Crown. The influence derived from the ma-nagement of the public revenue, and from the various expedients in the hands of the Crown, is fuch as commonly to fecure the fuccefs of every new regulation propofed by the Court, and to render

render the public deliberation little more than a matter of form. There are feldom wanting, indeed, combinations of individuals, who endeavour to oppofe the meafures of Adminiftration; but the efforts of thofe men, in ordinary fituations, have ufually no other confequence than to afford the entertainment of a debate, or at moft to occafion a little delay of the bufinefs. That this is the real ftate of the matter, is acknowledged by all the world; and while we reafon upon the nature of the Britifh Government, we are forced to admit that its operations, in this particular, are by no means performed according to thofe general principles upon which the political machine has been conftructed.

If what I have now obferved were to hold univerfally, if the influence of the Crown were, in all cafes, to over-rule the determinations of Parliament, it is evident that our liberties would be at an end; and that, fo far from maintaining the principles of the Revolution fettlement, we fhould be unqueftionably under the abfolute dominion of a fingle perfon. But in this, as in many other inftances which occur in the hiftory of the Englifh government, a remedy has been quickly provided, capable of ftopping the progrefs at leaft, if not of compleatly curing the diforder. From the very circumftances which produced this irregular exertion of Crown-influence,

C   there

there has arisen a method of controuling and limiting the extent of it, from which its dangerous consequences appear to be in a great measure removed. Though, from the concurrence of ordinary causes, the national assembly is commonly induced to follow the guidance of ministry, yet in peculiar circumstances a different disposition may prevail; and the conduct of particular Ministers may be so absurd, or of such a hurtful tendency, as to excite indignation and resentment, or to create a general distrust of their intentions. In such a situation, it seems to be the duty, as it is likely to be the inclination of Parliament, not only to reject with violence the measures which have been presented to their consideration, but even to require the dismission of those Ministers who have incurred their displeasure. To carry their views into execution, the House of Commons may refuse the supplies, and by suspending the operations of Government, render it necessary for the Crown to comply with their request.

If Parliament, on these extraordinary occasions, were only to refuse its concurrence to particular measures, allowing the Ministers to remain office, such a feeble testimony of its displeasure would be of little consequence. It would be of no avail in preventing ministry from acquiring the entire direction of parliamentary business. It would only

only teach them to change their ground, and to vary their method of attack; or to wait for particular conjunctures in order to accomplish a favourite measure. As the situations when a majority in either House can be formed in opposition to Administration occur but seldom, they must be employed, as often as they do occur, for the purpose of restraining effectually the improper exertions of the executive power. They must be considered equally in the light of a check to the past, and of an example to the future. To render the servants of the Crown cautious of abusing that extraordinary influence of which they are possessed, they must be convinced that it is impossible for them to retain their stations any longer than while they maintain the approbation and good opinion of Parliament. In short, as the Crown has manifestly encroached upon the free exercise of the Legislature, it is necessary that the legislative body, in order to preserve its independence, should make a corresponding extension of its privileges; and as Parliament submits in ordinary cases to be directed by Administration, the ministry ought on the other hand to possess the confidence of Parliament; and to be removed whenever they fall into a contrary situation. It is in this manner only, that the exertions of prerogative which I have mentioned, can be rendered consistent with any rational plan for securing

ing

ing the liberties of the people; and that the ancient balance of the conftitution, notwithftanding the various materials which have been accidentally thrown into either fcale, can in reality be maintained. '

The right of. Parliament, and in particular the right of the Houfe of Commons, to procure, by an Addrefs to the Crown, the removal of particular Minifters, feems, accordingly, to have been eftablifhed ever fince the Revolution. This is the doctrine that runs through the whole courfe of our Parliamentary Debates, and which has never been controverted, even by thofe whofe intereft it was to hold the oppofite opinion. Not a fingle inftance occurs, during that period, in which the defire of the Houfe of Commons in this refpect has not been complied with; and in moft cafes, when a Minifter has forefeen that an application of this kind was likely to be made againft him, he has thought proper to retire, in order to avoid the effects of it. Even in the earlier periods of our hiftory, we find the Parliament claiming the fame privilege, though they had not fo ftrong a plea to urge in fupport of it. The beft and wifeft of our monarchs appear, at all times, to have thought it incumbent on them to remove fuch Minifters as had incurred the diftruft and jealoufy of that affembly; and thofe who followed a different courfe, had, for the moft part,

occafion

occafion to repent of their indifcretion. Of the laft, the melancholy cataftrophe of Edward the Second, and of Richard the Second, and above all the unfortunate reigns of the Houfe of Stewart, are memorable examples.

It has been faid that the Addreffes of the late Houfe of Commons, in order to procure atten_ tion from the Throne, ought to have fpecified fome particular mifconduct in Minifters; and that the bare expreffion of their difapprobation, or want of confidence, was not fufficient to entitle them to a compliance with their requeft. According to my view, the reafon fpecified in the repeated Refolutions of that Houfe, appears the ftrongeft that can poffibly be affigned; an unconftitutional meafure of which thofe Minifters have been guilty in the very act which gave rife to their appointment. Does not this tend to excite ftronger fufpicions againft their political integrity, and fhow more clearly that they are unfit to continue in their offices, than if they had merely committed a miftake in the conduct of a war, or had been deceived with refpect to the productivenefs or popularity of any particular tax, or had fallen into any of thofe errors which are ufually infifted upon to juftify an Addrefs for the removal of miniftry?

I cannot help thinking, however, that the argument carries us a good deal farther. It appears

to

to me that the Houfe of Commons have pecu-
liarly a right to demand the removal of Minifters,
without affigning any fpecific reafon whatever.
As the Houfe of Commons are entrufted by the
nation at large with the power of granting fupplies, fo it is their duty to attend, not only to the
propriety of the taxes impofed, but alfo to the
proper application of the money which is levied;
and upon this account they ought, undoubtedly,
to be fatisfied of the integrity and abilities of
thofe perfons to whom the difpofal of the public
revenue is committed. They may often be
convinced, however, that particular perfons are
not qualified for fuch a truft, and yet be unable to charge them with any fpecific crime
or mifmanagement. The unfitnefs of any perfon for an employment of fo great difficulty
and importance may often become evident before
he has taken a fingle ftep in the execution of
that employment. Is it neceffary in fuch a
cafe, to fuffer the actual mifmanagement of
the public bufinefs, and to incur the hazard
of all the evils which may arife from folly
or wickednefs, before a remedy, fhall be provided?

But what I would chiefly obferve upon this
head is, that if the Commons are obliged to fpe-
cify a reafon for demanding a change in Adminiftration, their privilege in this refpect will be of

no

no value; as it will afford no check to the improper appointment of Ministers. If it is held necessary to assign a specific charge, in order to procure the dismission of Ministry, it will follow, that
what is alledged against them must be of sufficient
weight; for a weak or frivolous charge ought certainly to be as little regarded as no charge at all.
But who is to judge of the strength or weakness
of the reasons which are assigned in such cases?
Is it the Crown? That will be the same thing
as to commit the determination of the point to the
very Ministry themselves, whose removal is pro-
posed. An altercation, therefore, between them
and the House of Commons; a paper war, in
which the former will endeavour to justify their
conduct, and the latter to represent it as unjusti-
fiable, is all that can be expected upon such a
plan, whenever the Crown is disposed to support
the appointment of its Ministers. It were better
to abolish at once this privilege of the Commons,
than to make the people place any dependance
upon such a mere shadow of security against the
encroachment of prerogative.

From what has now been suggested, you will
be able to judge of the opinion which, I see, has
been of late maintained by Dr. Tucker; that the
only constitutional mode of removing our Ministers is by an *impeachment*. I shall only add, that
the Doctor appears not to have duly considered
the

the fmall profpect of fuccefs in impeaching Minifters who remain in the plenitude of their power;
that he has given no attention to the difficulty of
proving, in a court of juftice, thofe crimes which,
to the conviction of all the world, may have really
been committed by Miniftry; and that he has
totally overlooked the neceffity, which may fre-
quently occur, of removing a Minifter, on account
of his incapacity, his prejudices, or his pernicious
principles, when he has done nothing that could,
with propriety, be made the fubject of an impeachment*. The Athenians were fo fenfible of
the inconveniences attending the impeachment of
men high in office, that the people were permitted
without any trial to pafs a vote of banifhment
upon any perfon, how innocent foever, who had
excited

* This author has often delivered his opinien upon public
meafures; and his opinions are almoft as various as the
adminiftrations during which he has written. He was once
of opinion, that our exclufive trade with America was hurtful to the nation, and that, in found policy, it ought to be
relinquifhed. Upon another occafion, however, he thought
proper to juftify the American war, upon this principle,
that we had a *right* to fubdue the Americans. Public meafures, it feems, may be *legal*, which are deftructive to the
community. Change of circumftances may, perhaps, at
fome future period, induce the Doctor to maintain, that
though impeachment is the only *legal* method of removing
Miniftry, yet an addrefs to the Crown is the mcre *expedient*
one.

excited their jealoufy, and was accounted a dangerous member of the community.

The confiderations which I have laid before you, are fuch as can hardly fail, I fhould think, to arife in the mind of every perfon, who has had an opportunity of obferving our late Parliamentary tranfactions. You will recollect, however, that the reflections, which we have generally met with upon that fubject, and the views which have been held up in moft companies, are of a very different nature. The fact is, that inftead of bringing forward the great conftitutional queftion abovementioned to the examination of the people, the utmoft pains have been taken to keep it entirely from their view; thofe events, by which our fyftem of government appears to be deeply affected, have been regarded in no other light, than as they tend to promote the intereft of different individuals; and the attention of the public, during the prefent alarming and critical period, has been artfully diverted to fuch particular circumftances, in the conduct of the late Miniftry, as were calculated to excite popular clamour againft them. The chief topics of declamation which have been employed for this purpofe, and which appeared, for fome time, to engrofs the attention of different fets of people, were the *Receipt-Tax*, the *Coalition*, and the *India-Bill*. Concerning each of thefe, as the fubject has been

D   much

much canvaffed, it will not be difficult for you to
form a decifive opinion.

With regard to the *Receipt Tax*, it is natural to
expect, that after our taxes have been fcrewed up
to fo high a pitch, the great body of the people,
who are more governed by their feelings than by
refleƈtion, and who, by their fituation, are prevented from difcovering the neceffities of government, as well as the difficulty of procuring Ways
and Means, fhould be difgufted with a new ex-
aƈtion, which appears to fall indifcriminately
upon a multitude of people of the lower rank,
and is likely to ftare them in the face, in the num-
berlefs petty tranfaƈtions in which they are engaged. The propriety, however, and efficiency
of this tax, notwithftanding any inconveniencies
which were apprehended from it, appear now to
be admitted on all hands ; and it has accordingly
been voted for, and fupported by both parties.——

The date of this topic of clamour is now over ;
and the only circumftance relating to it, that feems
worthy of remark, is the uncandid behaviour of
that Minifter of Finance, who, at the fame time
that he approved of the meafure, was difengenu-
ous enough to conceal his fentiments, and permitted his adherents to make the introduƈtion of
this tax a handle for cafting odium and abufe upon
the late Miniftry.

The.

The coalition between Lord North and Mr. Fox has been the subject of so much discussion, that I would not wish to tire you with any obfervations upon it, farther than as it has been ufed by the oppofite party, to excite popular clamour againft the perfons concerned in that tranfaction.

When this coalition was firft announced to the public, it no doubt excited a good deal of furprize in the nation. The American war had given rife to two great parties, who approved or who difapproved of that meafure; and thefe were animated with much keennefs and refentment againft thofe perfons by whom the fuccefs of that war appeared to be chiefly promoted or oppofed;—when the American war came to an end, the fournefs and bad humour, contracted by the late ferment, were not immediately removed; and the different parties were ftill eager to gratify their prevailing paffions, by humbling the refpective leaders of the oppofite fide. How fevere and mortifying the difapointment therefore, when Lord North and Mr. Fox, inftead of fuffering that difgrace which the enemies of either had been treafuring up for them, were brought immediately into power, and became members of a joint Adminiftration.

The altercation at the fame time, which had taken place betwixt thofe different leaders, had been managed with uncommon warmth; and the oppofition of their fentiments had been remark-

ably

ably pointed. The nation seemed, upon that account, to suppose, that the public divisions between those two persons were to become the source of a private quarrel, and that the acrimony of particular expressions which had escaped them in the heat and violence of debate, was to rankle in their bosoms, and to produce a rooted personal animosity. But when we reflect upon this matter with coolness and impartiality, it surely must be acknowledged, that there was no good ground for entertaining such an opinion. Those who are the fondest of the British Constitution, will, perhaps, be willing to admit, that the keenness of debate in Parliament which it occasions, and the severity of censure which it encourages against Administration, is a small inconvenience which we derive from our happy form of government. It is a sort of tax upon good manners, which Englishmen ought to consider as the price of their freedom. But persons who are much conversant in Parliamentary debate, learn to estimate the expressions used on such occasions at their just rate. They make allowance for the intention of the Speaker; and they acknowledge the distinction, according to Parliamentary language, between the imputations thrown upon political conduct, and those which have a reference to private character. Indeed, without such a distinction, it would be impossible to sift, and bring to

light,

light, the conduct of Administration in such a manner as the interest of the public seems to require.

In any other view than what is suggested by the supposition of private resentment between those two persons, or between their respective adherents, their union, so far from deserving censure, appears to merit approbation. In the circumstances in which the coalition was made, this, or some other agreement, equally liable to objection, was necessary for carrying on the business of the nation.

The House of Commons was at that time divided into three great parties, who had been distinguished by their opposite opinions upon several very important subjects; and these parties were so equally balanced, that no one of them was capable, by itself, of executing public measures. Without a coalition between two of them, it was impossible to give consistency and dignity to the national conduct, by forming a strong and efficient Administration. But would it have been better, that Lord North should have coalesced with Lord Shelburne? or that the latter should have again united with Mr. Fox, whom he had formerly abandoned? The opinions, the political connections, the personal altercation, the reciprocal expressions of resentment or of contempt, which appeared to stand in the way of an union between

between Lord Shelburne and Lord North, were at leaft as confpicuous as any circumftánces of a fimilar nature which had occurred betwixt the latter and Mr. Fox. Was the charaĉter of Lord Shelburne fuch, as to create a firmer reliance upon his profeffions ? Had he appeared lefs aĉtive and zealous, in declaiming againft the influence of the Crown, or in turning out of office the fupporters of the American war? Yet there is hardly any man fo fimple as not to be firmly per-fuaded, that if Lord North had been willing to coalefce with Lord Sheburne, he would have been received with open arms, and this coalition would have been highly extolled, and zealoufly defended, by all the friends and connectins of that party, who now endeavour to reprefent the coalition with Mr. Fox in the moft odious colours.

But the India Bill, brought in by Mr. Fox, is the great circumftance which has given offence to a numerous and powerful defcription of peo-ple, and which has excited them to move Heaven and Earth in order to overturn a Miniftry, from which they dreaded the accomplifhment of a mea-fure that is fo obnoxious to them.

The diforders that have prevailed in the govern-ment of India are of fuch a nature, as cannot fail to awaken the compaffion and the indignation of every man who has perufed the authentic accounts of them, and whofe heart is not contraĉted and hardened

hardened by the strong, and often irrefiftible principle of felf-intereft. It is a melancholly prospect, to behold that fertile and extensive country, the feat of an ancient fyftem, of manners and of knowledge, the refidence of thirty millions of inhabitants, wafted and depopulated without mercy, and fubjected to all the miferies that can be conceived to arife from the lawlefs fury and rapacity of an undifciplined, and ill regulated body of mercenaries, directed and goaded on, by the unremitting and unfatiable avarice of a fet of merchants, or fervants of merchants, in whom, by long habit, every other feeling but that of avarice feems to be totally extinct. It muft be impoffible, one fhould think, for any member of the Britifh Legiflature to reflect, that he is, in fome meafure, acceffary to thefe depredations and enormities, without experiencing very painful fenfations, and without being difpofed to exert himfelf in putting a ftop to thofe evils. In the beginning of the prefent feffion, there was accordingly an univerfal cry for a ftrong and efficient bill, in order to correct the diforders, and to regulate the future government of India. No palliatives, it was faid, by the prefent Minifter, then in oppofition, would be fufficient; and nothing lefs was requifite, than a compleat fyftem of regulations, fuch as would operate a radical cure.

But

But when thefe were the general fentiments expreffed in Parliament, and throughout the nation,
the Eaft-India Company were meditating fchemes
of a very different nature; and nothing could be
farther from their thoughts, than to fubmit to thofe
intended innovations. In order to form an idea
of the motives and principles, by which their conduct, in this refpect, was directed, you will pleafe
to recollect, that the Proprietors of the India
Company are not to be confidered merely in the
light of a fociety of merchants, depending for
their fupport upon the regular profits of the
India trade. The regular and fair profits of that
trade are now, by neglect and mifmanagement,
reduced to a rate which is below the attention of
a great mercantile Company. The emoluments
derived from our intercourfe with that part of the
world, are chiefly fuch as arife from depredation;
and the *form of trade,* which is ftill kept up with
the country, is little more than the mode of re-
mitting the fpoils which have been amaffed by
illegal violence. The Proprietors of India Stock
at home are, of courfe, the real dependants of
their nominal fervants abroad. The dividends of
the former depending chiefly upon the fuccefsful
rapacity of the latter, both of them are excited
by the ftrongeft motives of intereft, to ftrain every
nerve in promoting their common-views. A
great part of the India Proprietors have, in fact,
purchafed

purchafed their ftock for no other purpofe, than
to fupport the intereft of the particular fervants of
the Company abroad, with whom they are con-
nected. To fuch Proprietors, any effectual meafure for regulating the government of India, muft
appear in the light of a propofal for draining the
fources of all their wealth, as well as for anni-
hilating their political connections; and a tame
acquiefcence in fuch a meafure can as little be
expected from them, as it can be expected from
the fervants of the Company abroad, who are
fattening upon the fpoils of India, and acquiring
immenfe fortunes, by which, when imported into
this country, they fhall afterwards be enabled to
fmother any enquiry into their moft atrocious
mifdeeds.

In thefe circumftances, it occafions no furprize, that the India Bill prefented to Parliament
by Mr. Fox, however well it might be calculated
for repreffing thefe diforders, was in the higheft
degree offenfive and alarming to the India Company. The more it was likely to be effectual in
promoting fo falutary a purpofe, the alarm which
it excited became neceffarily fo much the greater.
The utmoft oppofition, therefore, was made to
it in every ftage of its progrefs, by that numerous and powerful body of men; and the
moft outrageous and bitter invectives were poured
out againft it. When we confider, however, the

different

different arguments which have been stated in the course of this opposition, we find that they are altogether of a secondary nature; that they relate, not to the tendency of the bill, with regard to its main purpose, the government of India, (for in this respect it appears to be unexceptionable) but to the effects of it upon the state of the Company, and of the government at home. In this view, it has been represented as violating the *Chartered Rights* of the India Company, and as injurious to the *Royal Prerogative*.

As to the violation of the Chartered Rights of the Company, I can hardly persuade myself that the terrors which have been held out by so many people, and displayed with so much parade, are to be considered as real. The danger of trading companies, and to corporations in general, which some people appear to apprehend from the interference of government in regulating the affairs of this Company, on such an extraordinary emergency, I can regard in no other light than that of a mere bug-bear.

I must confess, indeed, that the reason, which I have sometimes met with in conversation, for interfering in the affairs of the Company, that, by their bad behaviour, they have forfeited their rights, does not appear to me a satisfactory one. It does not appear that a corporation can justly be be deprived of its rights, as a punishment for the offences committed by its managers.

But, surely, it will not be disputed, that the good of the nation, and the general interest of society, may afford a sufficient reason for restraining and modifying the rights of any individual, as well as of any corporation whatever. That the state has a right of regulating the property of all its members, with a view to the public advantage, has been universally admitted. It has never been doubted that Parliament may force a man to sell his ground for the purpose of making a turnpike road. The law by which heritable jurisdictions in Scotland were abolished, upon giving a pecuniary recompence to the persons thus deprived of their rights, has never been arraigned, as contrary either to justice, or to found policy. Even the Sovereign of the Isle of Man was, without any complaint, obliged, from considerations of public utility, to surrender his regal authority, and to accept of a reasonable compensation. The privileges of the India Company will not surely be looked upon as more sacred than the common rights of property. They are privileges derived merely from the positive interposition of the Legislature; and the establishment of them was, in fact, an encroachment upon the rights belonging to the other members of the community; an encroach-

ment

ment which nothing but the confideration of great public utility could juftify. At the fame time it ought to be remembered, that the pecuniary interest of the Company, fo far as it arifes from a fair trade, in confequence of their exclufiye privileges, would not, in any degree, have been hurt by the bill; but would, on the contrary, have been promoted, by turning the general attention from depredation to the ordinary profits of commerce. Nothing more was intended, than to regulate the trade and government of India, in a manner confiftent with the intereft of Great Britain, with the principles of humanity, and with the unalienable rights of mankind.

2. As to what is pretended that the fyftem of regulation propofed by Mr. Fox would have created a fourth eftate independant of the Crown, you will recollect that this pretence appeared to have little weight with any perfon, during the early ftages of the bill, though it was afterwards affumed with greater confidence, in order to ferve a temporary purpofe. The circumftance of the *Directors* of the Company being appointed by Parliament, inftead of being appointed by the King, cannot be thought to be of great moment, when it is confidered, that, in either cafe, they would have been really fuggefted by the Minifter. Neither would their being eftablifhed for a *certain period*, a circumftance neceffary to give energy
and

and vigour to their proceedings, render them independant of the Crown; since by the regulation propofed, they were to have been removeable by an addrefs from either Houfe of Parliament; and that the Crown might at pleafure procure fuch an addrefs, at leaft from the Houfe of Lords, no perfon who has been attentive to recent tranfactions will be difpofed to queftion.

It has indeed been argued, that, as the appointment of thofe Directors was to proceed from the late Miniftry, their friends would of courfe retain the government of India, independant of any future changes of Adminiftration, and the Crown would thus find itfelf hampered and limitted in the nomination of its fervants. This argument goes upon the fuppofition, that perfons who have obtained the independant poffeffion of an office will afterwards retain a conftant difpofition to ferve thofe individuals to whom they are indebted for their preferment. It fuppofes that they will be fo corrupted, as to make their public conduct fubfervient to the private views of a party, and fo virtuous, as to prefer the intereft of their benefactor to their own, whenever the former is brought in competition with the latter. How far this fuppofition is confiftent, or how far it agrees with experience, I leave you to determine. How far the principle of private friendfhip is likely to extend in politics, I fhall not take upon me to calculate.

calculate. But this I think may be said without offence: That suppofing a fet of Directors appointed upon the plan above-mentioned, their own intereft would concur with that of the public, in requiring that they fhould maintain a good correfpondence with any fet of Minifters who might hereafter be eftablifhed; and I fee no reafon to apprehend that they would be under much temptation to facrifice thofe important objects to the mere punctilio of gratitude, by the difplay of a romantic attachment to their old benefactors *.

In all thefe articles which have been objected to the laft Miniftry, we have an opportunity of comparing their conduct with that of the prefent Adminiftration. Both have approved of the Receipt Tax; but the difference lies in this, that Lord John Cavendifh, both when he was in office and out of it, had the manlinefs to ftand forth as the avowed fupporter of the meafure, wh le his fucceffor in office thought it neceffary to fculk and fhuffle, in order to avoid an explanation of his fentiments, and permitted his emiffaries to load the oppofite party with the odium of a meafure which he himfelf fecretly approved of. Both have produced an India Bill; but the principle which they adopted in their feveral bills was very diffe-

* I would by no means however be thought to degrade the ftandard of political gratitude fo much, as to refer you to the noted examples of Mr. R——n or Sir C—l W—y.

rent.

rent. Mr. Fox appears to have proceeded upon the principle of public utility, and endeavoured to produce an effectual fyftem of regulation. Mr. Pitt feems to have embraced the expedient of temporifing, and to have no farther view than of extricating himfelf from the prefent embarraff-ment. He fupported his bill chiefly by the *con-fent* of the India Company, who, as might be eafily fuppofed, were prevailed upon to prefer that fyftem which had the leaft tendency to re-ftrain the conduct of their fervants. What pro-portion of the India Proprietors concurred in giv-ing this confent, it is needlefs to enquire; for fure-ly, nothing can be more evident, than that no par-ticular members of the Company had a right, by a voluntary furrender, to give up the privileges belonging to the corporation. This is a point of law that appears to have been fufficiently under-ftood as far back as the reign of Charles the Second, when the boroughs were fo much mif-led to refign their privileges to the Crown, for the purpofes of promoting the defpotical views of the Court.

Laftly, We may turn our attention to the pre-fent *coalition* of individuals, by whom the conduct of Lord North and Mr. Fox, in this refpect, has been fo much arraigned. It is not a little remark-able that Gentlemen, who have complained of this meafure in others, fhould have fet an ex-ample

ample of fo fingular a conjunction in themfelves. Is it poffible for the whole compafs of nature to collect a more heterogeneous mafs of jarring elements, than go to the political compofition of what the poverty of our language forces me to call the prefent Miniftry. And yet they would make us expect that their union is to be productive of the public falvation. They have even modeftly told us, that, from mere motives of public fpirit, they could not think of refigning. When we fee Lord T——w united with Lord S—y, and Mr. D—s in a ftrict league with Mr. P—t, we may look for fomething extraordinary indeed——we may expect a new progeny upon the face of the earth—And perhaps it is reafonable to conclude, that the happy time is not far off, when the wolf fhall dandle the kid, and the fucking child fhall put its hand upon the den of the cockatrice.

Jam redeat virgo, *redeant Saturnia regna* —

I am, &c.

L E T T E R II.

MR. Fox's India Bill, mentioned in my laſt
Letter, how offenſive ſoever it was to the India
Company, and whatever clamour it might have
excited throughout the nation, would not, in all
probability, have effeſted a change of miniſtry,
had it not been for the concurrence of another
circumſtance, to which I muſt now beg leave to
call your attention.

That in Great Britain the influence of the
Crown has, for a long time, been gradually en-
creaſing, and this, from the natural courſe of
things, independant of the deſigns of any particular miniſtry, is the opinion, you know, of
many perſons; and for my part, I cannot help
thinking that it is well founded. There are two
circumſtances, reſpeſting the ſtate of the nation
in this particular, which I ſhall take the liberty of
ſubmitting to your conſideration.

1. The prodigious increaſe of the Crown revenue, ſo far as it has ariſen from an increaſe of
the number of people, by whom that revenue is
ſupplied, muſt infallibly, I imagine, have extended the influence of the Crown. Suppoſe

F   that

that a State is fo fmall as to contain only fifty thoufand inhabitants, each of whom can afford, in
taxes to government, to pay at an average twenty
fhillings; the revenue under the management of
the chief magiftrate, would, in fuch a cafe, be the
fource of very little authority. It would probably render him very little richer than feveral of
his moft opulent fubjeas; and as the fupport of
his dignity would require that he fhould live at
more expence than they, he could not be expeaed
to have any furplus remaining, to maintain either
a military eftablifhment, or a numerous train of
civil officers. If we fuppofe a nation fo large as
to contain five hundred thoufand free inhabitants,
and paying taxes in the fame proportion, the fo-
vereign, poffeffing a revenue of 500,000l. fterling-
would, by the management thereof, be raifed to
proportionably greater confideration and importance. As his income might poffibly be ten times.
greater than that of any of his fubjeas, he might,
after defraying the neceffary expence of his houfe-
hold, be in a condition to beftow a confiderable
fum for the mere purpofe of creating dependance.
He might maintain a fmall body of troops, to
ferve as a kind of body guard; and he might have
a variety of fervants and retainers in the feveral
departments of government. The authority of
fuch a Prince, however, could never be very great.

He

He could never afford to hire an army that would be able to subdue the inhabitants, nor to gain such a body of dependants as would be sufficient to counteract those combinations among his subjects, to which his tyranny might easily give occasion.

But if a State, instead of containing five hundred thousand, were to contain twenty millions of inhabitants, contributing at the same rate to the public revenue, it would be scarcely possible to prevent the Sovereign, who had thus the management and disposal of the annual sum of twenty millions, from establishing an absolute authority. He could afford to maintain, and the state of the kingdom would probably give him a pretext for maintaining, two or three hundred thousand regular troops; an army that would be master of the lives and fortunes of all his subjects. The multitude of officers necessary for collecting this revenue, the great variety of magistrates requisite for preventing disorders in so extensive a country, the great number of clergy, together with such as were employed at the public expence for the instruction of youth, the numerous pensioners and placemen, unavoidable in so large an empire, and whom the Sovereign would be in a condition to support; not to mention the still greater number of expectants in each of these departments: all these, having a constant interest to attach themselves to the fortunes of the Crown, would form such a powerful body

of

of auxiliaries, as, with their feveral connections, would produce an implicit fubmiſſion to every meaſure which the Monarch might be diſpoſed to enforce. In oppoſition to the wealth in the hands of the Crown, the property that could be accumulated by any number of individuals, united occaſionally for the defence of their privileges, would be little more than a drop in the bucket.

The wonderful increaſe of the public revenue of Britain, ſince the time of the Revolution, though partly owing to the increaſing wealth of the inhabitants, is at the ſame time derived, in a good meaſure, from the extenſion of her dominions, and from the greater number of people, who, in ſome ſhape or other, are ſubjected to the payment of her taxes. The loſs of America is to be conſidered, no doubt, as, in this reſpect, a great diminution of Britiſh ſubjects ; ſince the inhabitants of that country, from our commercial intercourſe with them, and by the monoply which we enjoyed, were in reality contributers to our taxes. But notwithſtanding the reduction of the Britiſh empire in that quarter, there can be no doubt, if we conſider its dependancies in other parts of the globe, and more particularly the ſubjugation of India, that it has, upon the whole, been greatly augmented ſince the period above-mentioned ; and the natural conſequences of this augmentation, by throwing greater weight into the ſcale of the executive

tive power, muft be obvious upon the flighteft re-
flection.

2. Another circumftance, which of late has
greatly contributed to increafe the power of the
Crown, is the effect of commerce, and of that
opulence which is derived from it, in breaking
down the old family connections, and in promoting a fpirit of venality and corruption.

In thofe times which immediately fuccceded the
Revolution, the nobility and great landed proprietors, though they had long been ftript of that
dangerous authority, which had produced a pre-
valence of ariftocracy in the early periods of our
government, were ftill poffeffed of fo much influence, as enabled them to collect and retain a number of faithful adherents, in fupport of every meafure in which they were warmly engaged. It was
therefore not difficult, in many cafes, to form a
powerful oppofition, the members of which were
not eafily feduced by the Court, to defert the flan-
dard of their refpective leaders. But the greater
advancement of trade has, in a good meafure, de-
ftroyed this hereditary influence, and has raifed
up to wealth and confideration, a fet of new men,
without connections, and without any principle of
union, but that which is directed by a regard to
their own intereft. Thus the great body of the
people, though they have acquired, perhaps, more
independance, and a higher fpirit of liberty, are

become

become lefs capable of profecuting any joint meafures for the fupport of their privileges.   They are
like an army without fubordination or difcipline,
incapable of availing themfelves of their own
ftrength, and eafily put into diforder, or cut in
pieces, by the fuperior fkill of the enemy. Among
a number of individuals, every one of which is
profecuting his own private views, the opportuni-
ties given to Miniftry of breaking every oppofition, by gaining thofe perfons whofe abilities or
wealth have rendered them formidable, may eafily
be conceived. In confirmation of what has now
been advanced, you will obferve that the late
elections have, in feveral places, exhibited a fort
of triumph of the inhabitants of towns, and of
the fmaller gentry, in oppofition to what is ufually
denominated the great landed intereft of the
country.

   To this circumftance, I am afraid, we may add,
the progrefs of that mercenary fpirit, which is the
natural confequence of great riches, acquired by
gainful employments, and of that neceffitous
condition which is often produced by habits of dif-
fipation and extravagance. In former times, thofe
who afpired to political confideration were generally actuated by ambition, at leaft, if not by motives of public virtue, and regarded pecuniary
confiderations as of inferior value. They were
excited by their birth, by their education, and by
                                        a con-

a confcioufnefs of their own dignity, to maintain
a confiftency of conduct. They were often tena-
cious of party principles, of their ancient connections, and even of their own particular humours,
opinions, and prejudices. How much the ftate
of the country has been changing in this refpect,
it would be fuperfluous to remark. Your own
obfervation will be fufficient to convince you how
univerfally the objects of ambition have been
made fubfervient to the fordid purfuits of avarice,
and with what fteady fagacity the defire of gain is
capable of perfevering on the trail even of petty
emolument. It would be an invidious tafk to
point at any recent occurrences, in order to fhow
how far the profpect of Court favour is capable of
altering public conduct, and of new modelling
public opinions. I only mean to take notice of
the advantages, which are thus obtained by Adminiftration, for bearing down every obftacle before
it, and in carrying all its views into execution.

In a fituation where the influence of the Crown
is gradually advancing, from the natural courfe of
things, we need not be furprifed that many individuals fhould find their account in profeffing a
warm zeal to promote its farther advancement;
and fhould be willing to affift in any meafures that
might be fuggefted for that purpofe. It is not
neceffary to inform you that the promoting defigns of this nature has been the uniform fyftem

of

of the prefent reign. We have too much reafon to believe that there are perfons who look upon the prerogative as too limited in this kingdom, and who think that there is no good reafon, why it fhould not be equally extended as in France, or in moft of the other European monarchies. Thefe opinions have been fometimes declared with fufficient opennefs; though, on other occafions, it is believed, they have been infinuated in a more fecret manner, in places where the poifon was moft likely to be attended with fatal confequences. If the American war had been fuccefsful, there can be no doubt that, by the great additional influence that would have refulted to the Crown from the government of that country, the fchemes of thofe gentlemen would, in a fhort time, and probably without much alarm or noife, have been fully accomplifhed. I am far from fuppofing, however, that every perfon who concurred in fupporting the American war, or even fome of thofe who took a principal fhare in it, had any the moft remote concern in thofe defigns. The truth is, the American war was fupported by a fort of delirium, which appears to have pervaded all ranks of men; and it is only when we have recovered our fenfes, and look back upon it from fome diftance, that we have become fenfible of the folly of our conduct. The iffue of that war, however, was not more favourable to the natural rights of mankind, than

it

it was fortunate for the liberty of this kingdom. It occafioned a total overthrow of thofe political meafures which had been profecuted for fome time; and it was the opinion of many that thefe would never be revived. For my own part, I acknowledge that I was led to entertain fuch hopes. But that thefe were ill-founded, the event foon demonftrated. The Miniftry, which was formed upon Lord North's refignation, had not been many months in office, before it became vifible that a powerful divifion of the C—b—t had been induced to defert the principles upon which they had rifen to popular favour, and to ftudy the advancement of their own private in-tereft, by fighting under the banner of preroga-tive. By the injudicious treaty of peace which they were conftrained to patch up in a hurry, thefe new adherents of the Crown were again defeated, and were left in difappointment and difgrace. It is not furprifing that they difcovered on this occa-fion the utmoft virulence againft the coalition ; to which their mortification was principally owing. Nothing now remained for the party, but to call in their forces, and to lie in wait for fome future opportunity of renewing their attack ; and this, as we have feen already, was prefented to them, by Mr. Fox's India Bill in the following feffion of Parliament. It feems to have been at firft expeft-ed, that this bill, from the noife that was made

G   about

about its tendency to *increase* the power of the Crown, would be rejected in the Houfe of Commons; from which the Miniftry would of courfe be overturned. But this having failed, a more defperate meafure became neceffary; and the dedefired event was with fome difficulty produced, by the unconftitutional interference of the Crown in the Houfe of Peers.

Even after the fuccefs of this meafure, a new Herculean labour was ftill behind, in order to reap any benefit from the paft. It was neceffary to gain over, from the laft miniftry, the greateft majority in the Houfe of Commons, which had ever, perhaps, fupported any adminiftration, in a queftion of fuch difficulty and importance. For accomplifhing this purpofe, two refolutions were taken; the nature and tendency of which deferved to be examined with the utmoft attention. The firft was to endeavour, by every artifice, to excite, throughout the nation, a clamour againft the former miniftry, and to procure addreffes in favour of the late change of adminiftration. The fecond, intended as a fupplement to the former, was to diffolve the Parliament.

With regard to the firft of thefe meafures, I fhall not difpute that cafes may occur which are fufficient to juftify an appeal, from the determinations of the Houfe of Commons, to the opinion of their Conftituents, or of the nation at large. As all government

government is ultimately derived from the people, so it must be understood that the people have a right to controul the exercise of those powers which they have committed to certain magistrates, or to certain classes and orders of men. But, on the other hand, it will certainly be admitted by every reasonable person, that these ultimate appeals to the people ought never to be made but upon very extraordinary occasions, nor without the most urgent necessity. The most important powers in the State are committed to the several branches of Parliament; and the Constitution knows no other way, but through them, of exercising those powers. Whenever Parliament is prevented from that exercise, there is an immediate suspension of all government. It is the duty of every member of Parliament to exercise the powers committed to him, according to his best judgment, and according to his conscience.——Though he ought, no doubt, to have his mind open to information from every quarter, and in particular to listen to the voice of his constituents, as that of men entitled to great deference and respect; yet the duty which he owes to the public, requires that he should be ultimately directed by his own opinion. A member of the House of Commons is not the representative merely of the borough or county by which he is chosen; he is the representative of the whole nation; and the voice of every county or borough in the kingdom is equally

entitled

entitled to his regard. The powers of government are committed to him, by the conftitution, for the very purpofe of avoiding that confufion, that ignorance, that inconfiftency, that endlefs delay, which would infallibly render the nation incapable of executing the moft common bufinefs, if the people were to affemble and take into their own hands the regulation of public meafures.

But if an appeal to the people ought, in all cafes, to be made with extreme caution, it is, moft efpecially, of a dangerous tendency when made upon the part of the Crown. It will not efcape your obfervation, that the late application to the people for procuring addreffes, in favour of Adminiftration, and againft the declared fenfe of a great majority in the Houfe of Commons, is perhaps the firft inftance of the kind that occurs in our hiftory. The complaints of the people, in former times, have been excited by a fuppofed union of Parliament with Miniftry, and have proceeded from a jealoufy that the national reprefentatives were too much under the direction of the Court. If ever there happens to be juft ground for fuch an apprehenfion, if ever Parliament fhould become fo corrupted as to betray the rights of the people to the intereft of the Crown, the whole nation muft be convinced that there is a neceffity or complaining But there is no great danger that complaints, upon that account, will ever become

come too frequent, or that popular clamour will ever arife to any great pitch without fufficient caufe ; for in fuch a cafe, the complaints of the people will be checked and counteracted both by the operations in Court influence, and by that of the leading men in the nation.

The cafe is widely different, when the Houfe of Commons and the Crown are at variance, and when the former is maintaining a point of privilege, in oppofition to a claim of prerogative by the latter. There it may happen that the clamours of the people fhould be excited by mere artifice, and without any juft foundation.

The danger of admitting the popular inter-ference, when procured in fuch a manner, muft be obvious. In the courfe of any important de-bate in the Houfe of Commons, the weaker party is tempted to lay hold of every circumftance cal-culated to fupport a lofing caufe. By joining their influence to that of the Crown, by application to thofe boroughs, or parts of the country where they have the moft immediate intereft, and by foliciting that part of the inhabitants who happen to favour their own views, it will be no difficult matter to procure addreffes, which, to thofe at a diftance, may appear to fpeak the langnage of the people. If an experiment of this kind meets with encouragement in one inftance, the example is likely to be followed in others ; and different fac-

tions

tions will be inclined in their turn, to support their own interest, by resorting to the same expedient. The Crown was formerly accustomed to carry on the great national business, by procuring a majority in Parliament. That is, doubtless, a method still. But another method will now be introduced, the peculiar invention of the present times; that of procuring a *minority*, by whose assistance, supported by such addresses as can be obtained, the same end may probably be accomplished. When the Crown is thus doubly armed, it must be a strong and obstinate majority, indeed, that is capable of resisting the efforts of prerogative.

But the dissolution of Parliament was the great resource of the present Ministry, from which they promised themselves the final accomplishment of their purposes. From the time that they came into office, there can be no doubt that this measure was resolved upon, in case it should be found 'necessary; but it was delayed for some time, and kept in reserve, for several very obvious reasons. It was thought adviseable to try every other expedient for procuring a majority in Parliament, before they hazarded a measure of such a desperate nature. In the mean time every art was practised, and every engine of corruption was employed, in order to gain or to intimidate those persons who disapproved of their late proceedings. It was necessary, besides, that matters
should

should be put into a proper train for the ensuing elections. Considering the state of the Constitution, it required a course of proper evacuations, and alteratives, to prepare it for that violent operation which it was about to undergo. Some little time was necessary for this purpose; and in order that the other party might be prevented from likewise availing themselves of this interval, it was requisite that they should be kept in suspense, with respect to the future dissolution. Intimation was accordingly given by the friends of the Minister, that he would not advise the dissolution of Parliament; an answer, confirming the same idea with regard to the intention of Government, was delivered from the throne; the Minister afterwards gave more positive assurances to the same effect; and, notwithstanding the earnest and diligent canvassing of ministerial candidates throughout the kingdom, the nation in general remained for several months in a state of uncertainty, concerning the final intention of Administration. Thus, when the stroke was at last given, which put an end to that Parliament, the Ministry had already done every thing in their power to secure the character and complexion of its successor.

That the power of dissolving Parliament is a branch of the King's prerogative is indisputable; though I believe, on the other hand, it will be

acknowledged,

acknowledged, that an intention to diffolve Parliament, merely becaufe the King could not procure a majority in the Houfe of Commons, has
not been harboured by any Englifh monarch from
the Revolution to the prefent time. The right of
calling the great national council was originally
beflowed upon the chief executive officer, becaufe, from his fituation, he was the fitteft perfon
to judge when there was occafion for its delibera-
tions; and he had, of courfe, the right of dif-
folving that affembly; which was nothing more,
than the difpenfing with its farther attendance.
It was always underflood, however, to be the
duty of the Sovereign to call meetings of Parliament as often as the bufinefs of the nation required it; and it was never fuppofed that he
would difmifs a Parliament, or refufe to call that
affembly, with a view of withholding public meafures from its confideration, or of diverting the
exercife of its powers into a different channel. —
The returning officer of a county, or of a borough, is entrufted, by the Conflitution, with the
power of returning the members of the Houfe of
Commons for his diflrict; but he is guilty of a
manifeft violation of his duty, if, in order to ferve
a job, he returns thofe perfons, who, according to
his beft judgment, have not a majority of the
legal electors. The branch of prerogative now
under confideration muft be viewed in the fame
light;

light; and the Miniflry are refponfible, if it has been perverted to any purpofes different from thofe for which it was originally beflowed.

That it has been fo perverted, however, muft be evident to the whole nation. Will any man pretend to fay that the laft Parliament was dif-folved, from the want of bufinefs requiring its determination? Is there any man fo hardy as to affirm, that there were not meafures of the higheft national importance preffing forward to the deli-beration of Parliament, and which could not be delayed, without extreme inconvenience, and even without the hazard of a public convulfion. Did the Houfe of Commons fhew any reluctance to carry on the national bufinefs; or did they not, on the contrary, demonftrate the ftrongeft deter-mination, ~~in fhort,~~ to facilitate and promote every meafure that might eftablifh public credit, and provide the neceffary remedies for the various exigencies of the State? Is there any man, who does not believe that the laft Parliament was dif-folved " merely becaufe the Miniftry could not otherwife obtain a majority in the late Houfe of Commons," and for no other purpofe than that of procuring, by minifterial influence, a greater number of friends in the prefent one? Will it be ferioufly maintained, that a diffolution of Parlia-ment from fuch motives, and for fuch a purpofe, is confiftent with the great ends for which the

H   Crowu

Crown was entrusted with this discretionary power?

The consequences, at the same time, of this measure appear to be pregnant with so much mischief, as must excite the most painful apprehension in every man who is anxious to preserve our happy Constitution.

To the Members of the House of Commons a dissolution of Parliament, at a time when the period of its natural expiration is at a considerable distance, must always be a serious matter. It was formerly the universal belief that our representatives, however they might be tempted by the prospect of Court favour, were in no danger of suffering any hardship from the displeasure of the Crown. This point was thought to be absolutely established at the Revolution, when it was provided, that no person should be called in question in any other place for his opinions delivered in Parliament. But we must now be content to receive a different doctrine. We have now an example set before us, that the House of Commons may be subjected to a very considerable punishment, if ever they shall persist in measures which are disagreeable to the Crown; they may be put to the expence of a new election, as well as incur the hazard of losing their seats: and this punishment may be repeated as long as their obstinacy continues. Without any disparagement to

that

that House, for which I entertain the highest re-spect, it will require an uncommon exertion of public spirit in its members, to preserve their readiness on such occasions, and to maintain their privileges, in opposition to the influence of the Crown, when backed by the terrors of an immediate dissolution. It will require, if possible, still greater virtue in their constituents, and in the nation at large, to support those members who have rendered themselves obnoxious to the Court, and notwithstanding the whole weight of the Treasury, and the various means of seduction, and of delusion in the hands of Ministry and their numerous adherents, to return them once more into Parliament. Such virtue, I am afraid, can hardly be expected ; and the effect of a dissolution, at least after one or two examples, will be such as every Englishman, who considers the matter with attention, must tremble to think of.

There are many well meaning people who seem to think, that though a dissolution of Parliament has been put in practice in the present case, it will not be extended to future occasions. But I cannot see the least colour for such an opinion. Will not the same motives which have induced the Crown to hazard such a step at present, produce a second experiment of the same kind, whenever there is a necessity for it, and whenever there

is

is any probability that it will be succefsful? Will not every Miniftry, in their own cafe, be judges of this neceffity; and be difpofed to think, that the accomplifhment of the particular meafures in which they are engaged, together with the prefervation of their places, are fufficient reafons for threatening a diffolution of Parliament, and even for putting their threats in execution? But there is ground to believe, that this latter ftep will, in a fhort time, become fuperfluous. It is reafonable to fuppofe that the fame members, who, by repeated ftruggles, have found themfelves unable to keep their feats, without ruining their fortunes, will at length be difpofed to quit the conteft, and retire into a private fituation. There can be little doubt, that the moft refolute perfeverance will be finally fubdued; and that the mere mention of diffolution will, in the end, be fufficient to overawe the firmeft minds, and to produce an univerfal and implicit obedience.

You will eafily fee that the Crown is thus likely to acquire what alone was wanting to eftablifh an abfolute and unlimitted authority. It was formerly underftood that the ordinary bufinefs of Parliament was pretty uniformly conducted by miniftry; but we always expected that, in extraordinary cafes, the Houfe of Commons, at leaft, would be able to make a ftand, and give a check to fuch meafures as were extremely improper. We muſt now, I ſuſpect, if we have not virtue to reſiſt the eſtabliſhment of this ſyſtem, bid farewell to theſe expectations. By the arbitrary exertion of prerogative, in the diſſolution of Parliament, the Houſe of Commons, it is evident, will be ren-dered of no more conſequence in the government, than a mere Parliament of Paris, commanded by the King, whenever there is occaſion, to regiſter the royal edicts.

I beg leave to add, that in ſuch a ſtate, our preſerving the forms of liberty, will only aggra-vate our misfortune. Our government will not only become an abſolute monarchy, but probably an abſolute monarchy of the very worſt kind that can be eſtabliſhed in a civilized and poliſhed nation. In France, where the Legiſlative, as well as the executive power, is openly and directly exerciſed by the King, there is commonly little danger from the abuſes of his prerogative ; be-cauſe the ſovereign and his miniſters are, in cha-racter and reputation at leaſt, reſponſible to the public. But whenever it happens, in any coun-try, that the great powers of government are exer-ciſed *apparently* by a national council, but *really* and truly by the Crown, the King and his Mini-ſters muſt be under no ſuch reſtraint; but will be encouraged to practiſe meaſures of which they would otherwiſe be aſhamed, by the conſideration that they are ſcreened from the odium and reſent-

ment

ment which their conduct is likely to excite. In a word the secret, and disguised exercise of arbitrary power, as it is more likely to arise in this country, so it is of a much more dangerous and pernicious tendency than that which is open and avowed.——

Such is the melancholly view, which I am sorry a regard to truth obliges me to lay before you, when you are just going to be initiated in public business. You are come to examine the result of that experiment which has been made upon the nation, and to discover whether it has been made with success, and with safety to those persons who have had the direction of it. Upon the behaviour of this Parliament, and probably of this very session, the fate of our government will depend. If the House of Commons shall be disposed to vindicate their privileges, and to show a proper resentment of the late measures respecting the dissolution of Parliament, there may be still a prospect that the dangerous wound, which has been given to the Constitution, may be healed. If, on the contrary, they approve of those proceedings, and discover a willingness to support the designs of Ministry, the dispute is over.

" Venit summa dies, et inclustabile tempus
" Dardaniæ"——

The

The knowledge I have of your political opinions, and the confidence I entertain that you
are much above any private confideration, which
a Minifter can hold out to you, leave me no
doubt of your line of conduct on the prefent occafion. There is one advantage, however, attending your prefent fituation. To difcern your
duty is not difficult, though the faithful difcharge
of it is important. You may alfo be affured that,
whatever mifreprefentations are circulated by the
tools of prerogative, every honeft and intelligent
man will approve of your conduct; and there is
the ftrongeft reafon to believe that, as the mift of
prejudice is every where beginning to be difpel-
led, the voice of the nation will, in a fhort time
be unanimous in feconding your efforts.

As to particular queftions which are likely to
come before you, during the prefent feffion, I
confefs that thefe appear to me of a more or lefs
confequence, according as they have an influence
in fixing the great conftitutional point which I
have mentioned. I have fome curiofity to fee
what fort of India bill will be brought in by the
Minifter, after the two former bills have been
thrown out, and after the public have acquired
fuch full information upon the fubject. That it
will be an effectual bill, for the protection of that
unhappy country, I have not the leaft expecta-
tion. Why fhould thofe men feek to reftrain the
despotical

defpotical government of India, who are feeking to eftablifh a defpotifm at home? Why fhould they endanger their places by encountering difficulties at a diftance, when the fuccefs of their operations depends evidently upon their avoiding any fcrutiny of their actions, and lulling the nation in thoughtlefs fecurity?.

The reform of parliamentary reprefentation is another object, which is likely to excite attention and upon which great profeffions have been made by the Gentleman who is now at the head of the Treafury. He is now in a fituation, in which his former promifes might eafily be fulfilled; and he may expect that the public will not fail to mark his behaviour. If a reform of parliamentary reprefentation was formerly conceived to be expedient, it muft now appear abfolutely neceffary, in order that the Houfe of Commons may be able to maintain its independance, againft the arbitrary power of diffolution exercifed by the Crown. But, in order that this meafure may correfpond to the views of the public, and be productive of thofe advantages which are expected from it, it muft be a real and a thorough reformation. It muft endeavour to ftrike at the root of the evil. It muft not be confined to the addition of a few county-members; while the numerous reprefentatives, elected by infignificant or by nominal and fictitious boroughs are permitted to

remain

remain in their former condition. To expect that the nation, in the prefent circumſtances would be contented with ſo ſlight an improvement, is to think that a hungry man will be ſa-tisfied with a mere *ſugar-plumb*. But it is needleſs to trouble you with conjecture about particulars which the delay of a few weeks will bring clearly to light. I ſhall therefore put an end to this long letter by aſſuring you, that

        I am, &c.

www.ingramcontent.com/pod-product-compliance
Lightning Source LLC
Chambersburg PA
CBHW022031080426
42733CB00007B/800